Perfect Imperfection

I Am, Who I AM

(Inspirational Poetry)

By Angie Reames

Pure Thoughts Publishing, LLC

ISBN: 978-1-943409-01-3

Table of Contents

Perfect Imperfection   **Angie Taylor Reames**

I want to first say I am grateful for each and every one of you. God is awesome. He is amazing and I am thankful that He loves me. I dedicate this book to my family. I dedicate this book to my husband for being the best husband that he knows how to be to me; loving me when I chose not to love myself. My husband for his commitment and willingness to stick around when I felt like I was going to lose my mind- for being the strength that I didn't have. I love him unconditionally because when he could've been just a man- he chose to be my superman. I dedicate this book to my children for seeing a flawless mom when some days I didn't deserve to be one- for loving me and taking care of me when I was at my lowest. I dedicate this to my parents and siblings because they always saw, ANGIE and loved me in spite of. I dedicate this book to Number 2 for always being my friend and loving me when I felt like I didn't need to be loved. I dedicate this book to my friends and to those of you who feel like you don't deserve to be loved. To those of you who need to be strengthened and renewed in your spirit. My prayer is that the gift that God has given me in some way blesses and encourages you. You are strong, you are beautiful, you have a purpose, God loves you and He hasn't forgotten about you.

My name is Angie Taylor Reames; I am the wife of
Antowine Reames. Together we have six beautiful children- Hannah,
Shakaila, Kalen, Antowine Xavier, Keenen and Keiara. Born on
August 14, I am my mother's baby and my daddy's only child. I was
raised in a single parent home by a mother who made sure we never
were without. As a child I always felt like I needed to be perfect. I
wanted to live the life as the Huxtables and be awarded for doing
well. I always felt like I was overlooked because I was the "good"
child and of course the ones who did wrong always got attention. I
have an older brother who seemed to get away with robbery and an
older sister who had a relationship with my mother that no one could
come between.

I can remember feeling like I had a life full of secrets. I
remember feeling like I could not tell anyone how I was feeling
because I always felt different. I would do everything to be perfect
so that I would get attention but it never worked. I wanted to sing on
the choir, I even tried playing the clarinet. I remember making the
volleyball team (everyone thought I should play basketball because
of my height-I chose to be different). I remember making the A/B
honor roll constantly, only to be treated normal. Looking back at life
now, I know that God had designed me differently. His thumbprint
was branded on my forehead and I had no clue.

I was not raised in a home where we attended church on Sundays. As a child, I am pretty sure I attended church less than ten times. My grandmothers attended church faithfully and I thought that their churches were the ONLY churches that existed. We would pass by other churches while driving, but it's almost like those churches didn't exist. On Sunday mornings, my mom would prepare Sunday dinner and blast gospel music on the radio. I remember hearing about God but never knew Him for myself. I always wondered why the people on the songs screamed so much and what "Hallelujah" meant. I was ignorant to Christianity. The image I had was, He was this giant that resided above the clouds. But God never took His hands off of me- I didn't know that then but I know that now. I began to love God, but He wasn't thrown in my life- I began opening my heart.

As I got older I would find myself praying when I wanted something. I believed that I was only supposed to pray when in need. I didn't know how to pray without asking for anything. I didn't pray every day or at all times. I never said grace or anything. I was taught that I should bless my food by my first born. She was enrolled in a Christian home based daycare and taught how to say grace there (Thank you Mrs. DD). As she would pray- I was encouraged that I should do the same. I would find myself going through the struggle of life and did what I was taught, turn the gospel music up on full blast- only this time the songs would minister to me. I have had the thumbprint of the Lord on my life- branding me before I knew Him but He knew me.

Please flip through the pages and I pray that you are encouraged. I pray that you are inspired. I pray that you allow the gift that God has given me to be a blessing to get you to your next level in who He designed you to be. I will share some of who I am throughout the pages of this book; you shall witness the truth in misery being ministry. God bless each of you.

Do you know who you are?

Hi my name is Angie Taylor Reames. I was born Angie Denise Taylor. I am a wife. I am a mother. I am a daughter. I am a niece. I am an auntie. I am a sister. I am a friend. I am my mother's baby. I am my daddy's only child.

I am a smile to friends in the midst of a storm. I am happiness to pain. I am shoulder to tears I am who I am.

I am a victim of depression. I am a victim of mental abuse. I am a victim of panic attacks. I am a victim of suicidal thoughts. I am here and I am a SURVIVOR.

I remember when I drank to wash the pain away. I remember when I carried blades to protect myself from me. I remember being in the club so that I wouldn't have to face the reality that waiting for me when I entered my home. I AM A CONQUEROR

I remember the night my lights got turned off. I remember when I didn't have money for lunch so I drank water to stay full. I remember when I didn't know how my ends would meet. I know the struggle. I AM ENCOURAGED.

I remember when I wanted to hear compliments from nobody's to make me feel like a 'somebody' and temporary romances that were temporary ignited flames existed because my self-esteem was so low. I remember laying there for his momentary affection after screaming no. I remember feeling torn and broken. I AM HEALED.

I remember being accused of everything except what He designed me to be. I remember being stuck between nowhere and the bottom- whispering to myself before I ran into hiding, saying no one loves you and no one cares. I AM STRONG

I often think of the days when I would plan my death only to snap back into reality of the children that I had given birth to would be left unprotected in the mess

I am guilty of doing too much for everyone else and not enough for me- never a relief. I am guilty of living in grief. BUT I am encouraged that my JESUS LIVES and He Lives in ME and I will share my story so that God gets the Glory because I don't want to be existing when I have been set free.

I am not what they want me to be. I am who He says I am. I am not what they think of me. I am who he designed me to be.

It took me to sit alone in a space occupied by loneliness and confusion. It took me to wallow and lay in a bed of depression and pain. I am here and I am UNDEFEATED.

I am not what they want me to be I am who I am.

I covered up my fears with hatred and I smiled when I felt intimidated. I laughed loudest when humiliated and when my cry was on the verge of escaping. At one point I actually cared about what other people thought of me… I wanted to be perfect. I wanted to be perfect for imperfect people just like you… just like me.

I wanted to be accepted- to feel a sense of belonging. I wanted to feel loved. When All along I was my mother's baby, my daddy's only child, and my father was doing all of what I yearned for, watching me from above. I was mourning for things that He hadn't designed in His plan. I was thinking about what I wanted and trying to get it from MAN.

I am not what they want me to be. I am who He says I am. I am not what they think of me I am who he designed me to be.

I have been a vault for so many who only shared what they wanted me to know in hopes that I would tell them something about me. So that they could run and tell that to others that they know… but I am no fool. I can trust me with you but I dare not trust everyone with my heart. Because all things that seem anointed haven't endured the process to be set apart.

Some have even tried to take my kindness for weakness and abuse the smile that I genuinely gave… just because I know Jesus doesn't eliminate the thug in me before I was saved.

The mother asked- Do you know who you are? Yes I do

I am not what they want me to be. I am who He says I am. I am not what they think of me I am who he designed me to be. I am not what they want me to be I am who I am.

I am not the clothes I wear. I am not the shadow of my eyes. I am not the gloss on my lips. I am not my hair and I am not my stride.

SO I ask… do you know who you are? With all the hell in our past. With all of the roadblocks on our journey. With all the mistakes that weve made. WE ARE Still here. Do you know who you are? You can use your past as your elevation. Don't sit back and hold a grudge for messy situation and people who chose to be fleshly septic tanks-filled with mess. Learn to forgive and begin to live. Your life is not your own but to God you belong. Reflect on you and know your purpose.

DO YOU KNOW WHO YOU ARE?

12/30/2013 ATR

I trust God and His plan for me

Sick to my stomach- frustrated and buried with **stress**. No matter how hard I pray I just can't shake this **mess**

The drama and the pain that keeps **attacking me- repeatedly** are disgusting and my conscience begins to **pity me.**

All these people continuing to throw rocks and stones and crush my **humanity** with their **belligerence**

I'm seeking God and crying for help but they keep **doing it**- turned to church because I thought it was **perfect**

But these people got issues just as me – and the preacher keeps saying press on the battle is **worth it**

I am trying to trust this God that I have never **seen** and have faith to what old people recite the size of a mustard **seed**

But how can I have faith and all the bad things are happening to **me**? I am just captured in spiritual **immaturity**.

Praying and Praying asking God to believe in **me** when it seems like everyone else has deserted **me**.

Alone and unaware of what this is that I am to **be**- Yet somewhere this old wretch will minister through **misery**

Because deep down **I trust God and His plan for me**

Why is it that everyone else seems perfect and I am here battling with **tears**- day after day year after **year**?

Decades of looking at life with my limited **perspective**- and dealing with people who see God in me but choose not to **respect it**

Targeted for my happiness when it seems to **show**- insecure in my walk with God- because I feel unworthy to others I **know**

Blind to my blessings from God because I thought my plan was **working**- but nothing spiritual is done fleshly – and I'm spinning wheels just **stuck here**

Preparing to do things and not consult with God- realizing some **things** don't go according to plan- not our plans without **God in…**

It seems that when my confidence is **released** and I trust Him- it's then that I know that what I do is for him and in his eyes he is **pleased**.

I am often motivated by the people who see my **flaws**- the people also known as the haters my inspirational motivators confirming my **call**

Even the scripture tells you about how Joseph's brothers hated on **Him** and God used Joseph to save lives and his brothers- he even saved **them**!

So when you think the devil is in your life- up to **nothing**… God turns it around for good and use the bad to produce great in **something**

You may be in a struggle and have no idea how the battle will **end**- But God wants us to trust **Him** because He knows what the ending will **be**

Because deep down like Joseph **I trust God and His plan for me**

So as hard as it may seem when you or I are going through hurt and **pain**

When it seems like we have nothing else to lose but with God so much to **gain**

When life gets despicable and everything seems to be going **wrong**

And we cry out to the lord in the storm—asking HOW long how **long**

Through the backstabbers and the naysayers- the he say and she **say**

When nothing we do seems to be right and nothing goes our **way**

When our families turn their backs on us and no one believes in **us**

Second guessing our every step because in ourselves we have no **trust**

But isn't it promising that our designer or creator still believes in **us**

So take a glimpse back over your life and realize that we were never left **alone**

He always gives us strength to endure when we trust Him- even when we are **wrong**

God always elevates us looking back He had every problem figured **out**

Whatever you are facing just know that with Him you are never **without**

There is a plan for your life- trust him to fulfill it- be the best you that you can **be**

Because deep down **I trust God and His plan for me**

1/16/2013 Angie Reames   Genesis 50:37-50

If you only knew how I struggled to trust God

Been buried in depression and pain- a dark place

Waited to be rescued- in what seemed to be a slow pace

Asked and prayed, prayed and plead

It's not what I want? - But it's what He says I need?

So I questioned my pleas and deepened my prayer

And when I didn't receive -my trust seemed to stray

If you only knew how I struggled to trust God

I have been lonely and disgusted- looked for an end

Searched for an outlet - gave my life to sin

Cried tears of abuse and screamed pain of what seemed like molestation

Bottled in all the pain of what birthed and raised devastation

Turned all of my trust into man- and relied on flesh

Went through the storms- did my thing- failed all the tests

If you only knew how I struggled to trust God

Guided by the wrong people led in the wrong direction

Stopped looking for long term love- just wanted temporary affection

Heartbreak that turned to anger and anger to insecurity

Insecurity turned to fear and fear birthed spiritual immaturity

Afraid to cry out to the Lord for help because I didn't want to be judged

So I cried tears of hatred for all the pain and I held a grudge

If you only knew how I struggled to trust God

Labeled as everything except what God designed me to be

Protected by a cold heart and eyes too blind to see

That what I thought was Faith only ended in Evans

Perfect Imperfection   **Angie Taylor Reames**

Wasn't worthy of eternal life- wasn't good enough for heaven

Living life in hell and leaning on my own understanding

And when confusion got chaotic life got challenging

If you only knew how I struggled to trust God

Wanted to be in control of something that I didn't give myself-

The gift called life and was too ignorant to go right so I got left

In the situations that I caused myself to remain in

Because I was afraid to have faith in a God that I had never seen

Why do I keep falling and continuing to fall short?

I questioned where I was and where I was going- things of that sort.

If you only knew how I struggled to trust God

This road hasn't been easy- but I am determined to stand tall

All of the chaos that I endured equipped me for this call

I am proud to say that I trust God wherever I come and go

It's through trust that our relationship with God grows

I refuse to rely on flesh and because God has my best interest at heart

But where would I be if I didn't have my past- and knowing now God was there from the start

But I must remind you- If you only knew how I struggled to trust God

Proverbs 3:5 Trust in the Lord with all your heart and lean not on your own understanding.

1/14/2013 ATR

I'm Crippled But I've Got A right to be here (the title came from a book that my Pastor wrote- with the same title)

You don't even know that I had to go through something to get to this place

But yet you judge me and label me with what you think you know about me- say I am a disgrace

You have no idea that I am doing what I do because I was taught how to be a survivor

And church folks so quick to look down on me so I run to Lodebar- and go into hiding

I felt neglected by the people who I actually thought were supposed to be my friends

Because they always took, took, took and they began accusing me of awful things

That I lived up to- I was told that I would never amount to anything and I felt like I wasn't worthy to be a Kings kid

But even with all the dirt that I have done- I still got dusted off-I'm a living witness- look at what God did

So even through my struggle- I'm stronger with each tear-

You don't know my story, But I'm perfectly aware that **I'm crippled but I've got a right to be here**

Honestly, I began running from who I was designed to be

Because I believed there was no way that God would use a wretch like me

I started believing the negativity that was cast in my direction

Ran to momentary love, shotgun affection and pretended satisfaction

Relayed that the world was my permanent address

Settling for temporary love, momentary affection just for my pain to digress

Drank to erase the pain of what life had given me for quick crutch

Even sat on the corner and hung with the fellas to get a puff of the Dutch

So even through my struggle- I'm stronger with each tear-

You don't know my story, But I'm perfectly aware that **I'm crippled but I've got a right to be here**

Perfect Imperfection   **Angie Taylor Reames**

I'm not surprised at the things that God can do- I believe in His word
and I trust it to be true

But if you knew all of what I did back then- would you love who I
am now- and all that I went thru

So many Attempt to be so politically correct and perfect in every
aspect of this religious personification

While we sitting in church, meddling over petty stuff and souls are at
stake in the lost generation

I could've been dead a long time ago but somebody believed in me
enough to pray for me

So why should we let Phibe be lost just because we putting others
down in the name of Jesus- Spiritual Blaspheme

Who said that any of us were perfect- But God still thinks we're
worthy- So who are we to judge what the next man did

When there are people out here dying from lack of spiritual
nourishment but if we get them and bring them to the Fathers table
they can live

We got people out here turning tricks to make a dollar

And we judging instead of trying to be a role model

Women getting abused by guys who don't know how to be men

Perfect Imperfection   **Angie Taylor Reames**

Staying in situations, being manipulated by material things

Children getting molested by mama and daddy's lovers

And we too caught up in our ways to go help others

We all have a story, a background and history- so why can't we help the lost generation- they just like you and me

We all have sinned and fallen short- But I refuse to sit back and watch the God vision in Gods people be a subject of the world's abort

So even through the struggle, we must remain strong with each tear-

 You don't know the story, but we are all aware that **we're crippled but got a right to be here**

5/30/2013

Church announcements- Titled: Army Rising UP dedicated to Pastor Andre' C Barnes

Who said it had to be a list of current events or flyers with what's to **come**

What if I stood here this morning and gave you a run down on everything that God has **done**

For us as a church family in this season- the journey had some unexpected **turns**

But yet the journey is necessary for us to grow and be obedient to the lessons that need to be **learned**,

So what is the purpose of complaining when we've all experienced a season of **mess**?

Clean yourself up, stop focusing on everything negative and endure your anointing- it's a **process**

See a year has passed and we are here at the first Pastors Anniversary Celebration for **Dre**

And a year ago we were babies on this journey not even expecting to get to this **day**

Anticipating everything that surrounded us personally, praying that life didn't have to be so **hectic**

Wanting to run to the arms of the church, losing focus of ourselves and blaming others when we felt **neglected**

If *leaders lead* then you must first lead yourself or you'll be stuck losing everyone **else**

I stand here today honored to call Andre Barnes my Pastor because in this year he has given his **best**

I find it to be an absolute blessing to have a *covering* that I can truly say is **loyal**

He may not say everything I want to hear at times but he encourages me before my face hits the **soil**

Just a few announcements on what Pastor has **confirmed**

Because see there is wisdom in everything that God blesses and I am willing to **learn**- Listen

Who can confirm were different out of lyrics from *2 chains* and help us to realize we're better with lyrics from ***drake***

So we started from the *bottom now were here*- scarred, bruised, bent but we didn't **break**

So to our Pastor I say I think the *glass i*s starting to fill, half full or half empty- we must fill the glass

No looking back, sometimes you got to *lose to win*, and there is nothing new in our **past**.

And even with the present –you *can't handle me like you last saw me I ain't about that life- no not this* **time**

See I am the vision, God has revealed, directed, protected and corrected and I ain't got no worries victory is **mine**.

Thinking I was unworthy but now I'm perfectly aware that if *God called me to it that he will* **provide**

He has a plan for us- yet we so *dumb we sin and from God we try to* **hide**.

Call me Mary J because I declare and decree I am stronger with each **tear**

Or call me Mephiboseth because I am perfectly aware *that I am crippled but I've got a right to be* **here**.

See Pastor I've seen you preach funerals and touch lives and witnessed souls being **saved**.

I know you had to be God sent, Salvation is not the move the devil **played**- check mate

You have instilled in us that leaders are supposed to lead, so why would I want to be less **anyway**

I've learned that *forgiveness isn't for the other person*, it's for me forget the games that people **play**

You continue to push us to *be our best self*; only a fool would be content in a circle and settle for **less**

So to the church I say- *It's time to take your place at the table*- There are great advantages to being *leftovers*

And to Pastor I say Happy Anniversary, because even for you the *pain is gone but you must be a little **sore**.*

I stand here today briefly confirming these church announcements for Rev Andre C Barnes Senior, Pastor of the **Mount**

I say to you don't ever grow weary in your well doing- *Do you know when the Lord speaks*? He has never counted you **out**

Whether you're at Lake Murray preparing for a message, on a walk trying to clear the fog from frustration, whether you are trying to regroup knowing that God is in control, Doing a Community Revival for the Catholic Church in Kentucky, Preparing for Bible Study, seeing about others or meditating... don't grow weary in your well doing.

Stress makes you believe that everything has to happen right now. *Faith* reassures you that everything will work out in Gods timing.

Wish IT- Dream It- Do it... God has a plan for you. I am just glad He gave us The Mount Hermon Missionary Baptist Church family the opportunity to be a part of it.

I can't give an autopsy report of a dead church- because these bones can, shall and will live. We've come too far... we won't be defeated. We are the ARMY RISING UP! Happy Anniversary Pastor,

This ends the Announcements. Angie Reames 09/11/2013

When there is a thumbprint on your life- of course that means there is no doubt that there is a purpose. When I was ten years old I was almost molested by someone who was very close to my family. I trusted this person with everything in me and one night he treated me differently and asked me to do something that I knew would lead in the wrong direction; I ran. I remember holding it in until I was about sixteen. I never wanted to tell anyone because I didn't want anyone to look at me like it was my fault. I didn't anyone to blame me because I love him, but apparently he loved me in another way. When that happened at the age of ten, it transformed me to live a life of secrets. I just didn't trust anyone. NO matter what I did, I would keep it to myself. Assuming that the safest place to keep anything that concerned me was within. Holding everything in scarred me because when others would hurt me I never shared it with anyone because I was afraid. I have been abused mentally, physically and emotionally. Happy in situations that I labeled relationships because giving me to them made them happy yet my feelings were never considered. I didn't know my worth. I have felt like I didn't deserve to live. Refusing to tell anyone my struggles; because as a child I just wanted to be viewed as the perfect person and that apparently never changed. I would take matters in my own hands and handle them best way I knew how… with anger, bitterness, resentment, alcohol, blades and curse words. I have even considered suicide, which resulted in more stress that led to panic attacks. Panic attacks made me feel like I was crazy, like I was losing my mind. I began blaming everything that concerned me on the devil. Senselessly, I fell into depression and at night I would cry myself to sleep thinking about everything that had happen in my life. Positive things in my life were irrelevant to my mindset, I was so busy focusing on the negative things that occurred and never looked at the fact that I was still alive. I am a conqueror despite all the hell I have been through.

I can recall after accepting the Lord as my Savior, going to the club and feeling completely out of place. I recall placing myself back into the chapters of my story in my book, revisiting places that I had already passed. Now don't get me wrong, I did/am not assuming that I am better than anyone but I am saying that I am better off than a lot of the things I was allowing to come back into my life. I tried to avoid my purpose because it stunned me that God wanted to use me, in my mind, I wasn't good enough. I remember when I would depend on a knife for protection and alcohol to erase the pain. But it was only temporary. I know that I am chosen by God and I am grateful. I know that now. The same things that I enjoyed (my talents) before I was saved I do them for HIM now... I minister through poetry and dance (my gifts). I wake each day delighted to be a soldier in the army of the Lord. Don't let your current situation or your hell state make you feel like you aren't worthy of His goodness.

My Baby is Kicking

There is nothing more thrilling than experiencing the birthing of a vision dreamed by a great theologian and casted on the people and the vision must be birthed because the baby is ready to be revealed and even in its final trimester the kicks seem so surreal. So here we are in 2014 birthing the vision and celebrating with the man of God the God sent servant of this house because it's time to push because the vision has to be birthed. See you may be **crippled but you've got a right to be here** and even if you must encourage yourself the pain from the race is evidence that it's all worth-the lesson is life changing. Remember- *the teacher doesn't show up until the students are ready*- and when silence is evident- the pain is still steady.

2014 the birthing of the vision- 14 the year of double spiritual perfection and anything worth having is worth giving and **stretching out your other good hand** because if you are anointed you don't have to announce what God has already given- blessings- remain soaked in humility knowing **you aren't all that**. Without God you remain complacent in your pity parties looking for spiritual epidurals to alleviate your contractions- well what's the purpose of **looking full and living empty** not knowing your purpose- you may be connected to the **right train but rolling on the wrong track** and content in your flesh singing because **I'm happy** when in the spirit God blesses those people who depend on him for all their grief in its large raft.

Before I let go- I don't want to live here **reaching for false expectation knowing that they only lead to internal frustrations-** I know that **there is more to life than this** and even others can roll down the streets in the same city that I reside in and get pregnant in the spirit – immediately suggesting that we *download the install- it is necessary to have a new processor to have the download* but some don't even realize that **one man's junk is another man's treasure- be grateful for what you have and careful what you throw away** because one may *see drunks that are actually deacons, crack heads that are actually ushers, pimps that are actually preachers, thugs that are full time security,* just because we are in this building doesn't mean we are the only one with a testimony and even when **pretty hurts** realize that we must reach beyond the walls because even our cries are- **you don't know me you don't live on my street** and the unpredictable truth is knowing that **you've got more than you know-** you were born with a purpose- placed in this earth- and when you become **connected to that which you must kill** – knowing that personally- **I'm still here- taking my life back, turn down for what** when the strength of the Lord dwells within me-

So I'll repeat -There is nothing more thrilling than experiencing the birthing of a vision dreamed by a great theologian and casted on the people and the vision must be birthed because the baby is ready to be revealed and even in its final trimester the kicks seem so surreal. So here we are in 2014 birthing the vision and celebrating with the man of God the God sent servant of this house because it's time to push because the vision has to be birthed. See you may be crippled but you've got a right to be here and even if you must encourage yourself the pain from the race is evidence that it's all worth-the lesson is life changing. Remember- the teacher doesn't show up until the students are ready- and when silence is evident- the pains is still steady and inside the wounded comforters still seem a little giddy.

And we've arrived at the Birthing of the Vision and the 2nd Pastoral Anniversary of Our pastor- Andre C Barnes… The Baby is Kicking- And this is your welcome.

Angie Reames

9/12/2014

Adept at Adapting

I see you.

Constantly getting judged for just being you

Just when you thought you were real, your spirit gave you truth

The whole truth and nothing but the truth, lies beneath your external,

Everyone so busy looking at your outside and missing out on your

internal

Circumstances that surround you at your core,

The pain and suffering seep from you and your inabilities pour

Out of you there are great works that God will command

You have and you will continue to give it to God and then stand

You are just so **Adept at Adapting**

I see you.

Struggling to change your inner circle

Of friends that haven't helped you get where you need to be as a

man

So you step out on faith instead of taking matters into your own hand

Allowing the spirit to guide you and the flesh to lose

While you are growing the naysayers are still judging and looking

like fools

You know when it's HIM you proclaim that the feeling is different

Your language becomes powerful instead of belligerence

Your persona is astute and your head is held high

You are finally starting to realize you're an awesome child of God

You are just so **Adept at Adapting**

I see you.

Growing for you and not because someone ask you to

Be someone you aren't when you are wonderfully made

By the hands of God, this ain't no act this ain't no parade

I won't allow anyone to rain on your happiness or joy

Especially when you put it on blast and end by saying that is all

You are working on that inside job, your interior circumstances

There is no better time than the present for Spirit filled advances

You are skilled and perfect at being you

You're even the VP of the Goof Squad Crew.

This is the beginning of something phenomenal

Whether you are Bill, B, Brandon, VP or Pablo

You are just so **Adept at Adapting**

This one is for my great and awesome friend Brandon "VP"

Lewis!!! Blessings to you in your growth process! Love you B!

                                              Your friend

Angie T. Reames 4/19/2012

And then Stand

It's another one of those things of insignificance
Another one of those things that we seem to make major

The little thing that we have blown up to make a situation magnify
It's another one of those things, micro that we've made life size.

Complaining about how our kids are misbehaving,
When part of the problem is the lack of something that we have
created.

We're pouting about how that man has done us so foul,
When the issue is we're looking for that man we didn't have as a
child,

So actively trying to fill in that space, that emotional neglect,
Not realizing our plans don't work and God ain't finished with us
yet.

We're so busy rushing to make our fleshly relationships so
successful

Perfect Imperfection　　　　　**Angie Taylor Reames**

When we call on God because of religion and not in the spiritual,

We're stuck on ourselves, forgetting what we've came through,
Trying to create chaos in our present from pain in our past
Because we know how our sin relationships always meet and then crash
Constantly looking for attention and ministering for our wrongs
When in actuality it's a repetition of the same mess that has been going on too long, so…

Now it's trying to justify the wrong we've done to be right,
Because we still haven't learned that we are to walk by faith and not by sight.

Pointing our fingers and blaming it on others, wanting help on fixing the situation,
When we can't forgive our self for our problem, we just looking for an explanation,

Looking for forgiveness for our self-inflicted wounds,
That love hate relationship for character, that creating of self-doom.

Generating something major because we think our issue is different,
When it's the same problem in disguise - which we have dressed it up with.

Now we're looking for pity and life in all the death places,

Head hanging low, broken hearts and long faces.

Let's grow and get ready for this shift; it's a transition in this

season...

I know that God answers prayers in his Time and for his

reasons...so....

At this moment we stop looking for all the answers

From everyone who has nothing to do with the issue at hand,

All because we're too busy magnifying the micro instead of giving it

to God... and then STAND!

4/9/2012 Angie Reames

Christians and Church Folk

You continue to damage your vessel

Combining what is Godly to what you think is right

Becoming a distraction for the ones who believe in Christ

Yet we pray harder because there is a distinct difference between
you and me

Believe in the Bible and you believe in the notes you jotted down on
a committee

Based on colors and a speech with the wrong man to deliver.

Who died and appointed you God? Concerned with the program and
not your program

Or should I say your prerogative. Afraid to hear God, because you
are what we call they.

I am just trying to tell you… there is a difference between Christians
and Church Folk

Now come along my friends come along get aboard and ride this
train

You choose to sit on the bench and look at us prosper because you
assume you have nothing to gain

The devil is a liar if you think your life is perfection

It's your wicked ways that have caught up with you and your slave
mentality transgressions
Stop allowing your past to attack your present
Missing out on blessings because you too busy trying to get
recognized
Or is it that you are afraid of what maybe publicized.
Destroying your appearance to everyone else, messing up your
character, destroying your pride… did you stop to think that your
crap was still visible in Gods eyes?
I am just trying to tell you… there is a difference between Christians
and Church Folk.

Now you try to belittle my growth in the master,
Because I am learning more about Him and the promises waiting.
Worried about the building that your ancestors built, I'm stating

My soul is more important than the bricks, around your house is
dirty
But you continue to try to sweep around mine, I'm in the word,
you're just worldly
Gain nothing, if you have No God, and yet you continue to please
man
All to be leader and recognized in the small town hall of fame.
I'll leave the people right where they sit,
I got some more feeding to eat and a lot more Jesus to get.

I am just trying to tell you… there is a difference between Christians and Church Folk

I am praying for you to open your eyes and know

That God is about to move: It doesn't have to include you but will be in your best interest

How can you not want to grow?

Rather judge us and attempt to make us your foot stool

So I ask again… who died and appointed you God?

I have been saved and serving is what I will do.

Called or chosen, my works are not done for you.

You will fall if your plan is not for HIM

Continuing to get caught up in church affairs

Let your legacy be phenomenal, do you look like heaven or hell?

 I am just trying to tell you… There is a difference between Christians and Church Folk.

Angie Reames 2/23/12

Don't ever grow weary in your well doing!

This poem is dedicated to Pastor Andre Barnes

You came, you saw, you conquered. You saved.

You are here, you see, you won. You save.

You help, you claim, you love. You lead.

You make the weak see what the blind man desires to believe.

The people said the house was divided and yet others are adapting to be on one accord.

Because when we enter we come to worship, we depart we go out and serve.

You claimed and achieved when some slandered you and thought you were unfeasible

The people gathered and prayed, believed in you, Christ said you're redeemable

What man thought of you was irrelevant, to what God had already planned

Your anointing is greater, your faith made you strong and the fight made you stand

Perfect Imperfection   **Angie Taylor Reames**

Even when you were tired you were focused to endure, because the results would be worth it

God had spoken, you know, Herod may have a plan but God has a purpose

Come on Warrior Dre, Uncle, Bruh… ok Pastor Barnes, rejoice now Soldier, you've won

Wake up; It's time to Come Out, God never said it was over, the people just called it done

You have survived the chaos; it was crazy because it ironically became the norm.

You Warrior Beast, leader of leaders… you minister to us and tell us to go feed em

This transition is just the beginning of a beautiful transformation; I'm calling on His name

Jesus, Jesus, Jesus… because after this season, no one will be the same

Don't kill me baby, you have a dream and you got us to cast our vision

I've got to have HIM, God gives us choices and you minister to us so we make the right decisions

I've learned that it's ok to love the Lord and Live at the same, same time

It's ok to be different and spiritual at the same- same, time, People having fun as Christians and Growing at the same, same time, no crime.

Pastor Barnes there is greatness in you that shows through us, Called or Chosen that greatness is Power

I'm falling and I can't get up or can I? God ain't done, you're about to go higher

Activate Dreams; activate visions, all the hard times that you experienced were a compliment of the devil

So Arise Come Forth… Where is the enemy now? He doesn't belong on your level!

Don't ever grow weary in your well doing.

Angie Taylor Reames 7/9/2012

Revised on 7/16/12

I am a Child of a King... I am ROYALTY

Is it obvious? That the pain has crippled me and I not even know

Is it evident? That the bruising isn't invisible & every mark now shows

Is it apparent? That the fear is no longer internal but everyone sees

Is it clear? That the excuses aren't justified and you keep hurting me

The constant reminder of you continuing to batter my soul

The repetition of the heartache and the dignity that you stole

The lies that I've told because I just can't let go

I continue to allow you to abuse me and I'm drained

My blood is no longer flowing thru my veins and this pain I can't sustain

My spirit has died... I'm just trying to maintain the sanity that is no longer in me... or is it

Well it's important that I proclaim I WON'T TAKE IT... NO MORE"

I have protected you long enough because you say you love me

Perfect Imperfection   **Angie Taylor Reames**

I'm tired of defending your weakness when you keep abusing me

But you say what I need to hear when I need to hear it when I can't fear it I just tear it

You compliment me on the eyes, the same ones that that you hit me in

And tell me how you like my stride, when you just kicked me in my

Assume that I am going to be around to be your filthy rag

But my body is battered and my hair looks like a hag, my clothes are dirty, but they are packed and in the bag, I know I need to leave

But when I tell the world my story, I'm afraid not one person will believe it

So I cover up with the garments that you purchased, because you said that no one else was worth it.

And I was foolish to accept your gifts because you apologized when I lied, ashamed of the black eye and protectant of your pride, so I abide by your rules

I keep telling myself that no one will love me like you do. You have made me your absolute fool.

Afraid to look in the mirror, see these eyes have allowed you to damage the innocence that I had. Now it's dark I'm still in love with

The idea that you care but you have taken the happiness I had- now I am always bitter and mad

Well it's important that I proclaim I WON'T TAKE IT… NO MORE"

Your abuse is your tongue the way you curse me. Your abuse is your eyes the way you watch me fall.

Your abuse is your hands the way you hit me. Your abuse is your foot because you kick me when I crawl.

Your abuse is the way you touched me. When I trusted you with everything in me. You took my life.

Your abuse is you taking advantage of my strength and making me mentally, emotionally weak

Your abuse is your broken promises. I'm fed up. I'm fed…I'm fed up with it all

I won't let you continue to cripple me. I declare and decree that you won't hold me hostage.

I am free… I release and if you don't understand English I can give you Greek- Balo- I forgive you…

I'm the victim... I am the victim of someone else's problem... I am the victim of someone else's pain

I feel like I am losing in this battle, beaten by heartbreak, nothing to lose and nothing to gain

Just stuck mentally right in that place where they took my identity, and looked me in my face knowing I wouldn't tell a soul- can't release because my voice they stole.

Destroyed my happiness and shattered my innocence replaced it with anger, hatred and bitterness.

But yet You say I am to forgive.

How many times am I to forgive? And Lord you say~ seventy times seven.

I'm the victim... I am the victim of someone else's sin.... I am the victim of someone else's insecurity

I feel like I am losing in this battle, buried by an emotional barrier, imprisoning my personal maturity

I am mentally stagnant; abandoning the little of me that I know... but I was told with forgiveness comes growth.

So I will forgive you ~ it's time that I release... AN apology is one thing but we all need to forgive. I am no longer intimidated by your status; I am no longer a fool to carry this baggage. I refuse to be your victim- I deserve more...

Well it's important that I proclaim I WONT TAKE IT...NO MORE" Stop allowing someone to abuse you because you won't forgive. Abuse... Not ME, Not YOU, O NO WE WON'T TAKE IT NO MORE--- I forgive you... I release... I am no longer ashamed... I am a child of a KING and I am ROYALTY.
6/16/2012 Angie T Reames Revised 12/18/12

I am not perfect... But saved with issues

You look at me and you see happiness.

I look at me and see flaws.

I want to be able to laugh without comedy and

Cry without drama... No Pain

Will come from my heart if I don't allow the enable to enter

So now because of it you look at me and see fragile

When it's just my emotions are unstable and my heart has been

battered,

I am not perfect... but saved with issues.

My pillow are stained from the results of broken peace

A setback that resulted in a glorious comeback

Yet me trials are still trophies on my shelf

Funny how the good things fade and bad memories are left

Without of trace of my happiness that I once held dear

Learning to let go of my past, in my future I saw fear

I am still engaging in that closer walk with thee

I am not perfect... but saved with issues

It's crazy how the enemy will attack when you are your lowest,

You know better and are expected to better, where is your faith

Perfect Imperfection   **Angie Taylor Reames**

How can you allow this to take place? I keep asking myself…
Who can I run to when I need love? I always listen, I always care…
I am just a broken vessel in need of minor repairs.
My tear stained face… eyes of weariness and heart of despair.
I give myself away so you can use me
I am not perfect… but saved with issues.

Finding guilt buried in my heart for things out of my control
Learned to forgive myself of my past but the pain I can't let go
It's easy to forgive but how do you forget
Imagined where I would be if my past hadn't happened to me yet
The mental bruising a reminder of my battle
The war between myself and me
You see my smile, I feel my pain, I walk the walk, and Jesus has the plan
I am not perfect… But saved with issues.

I could stand her and give you a life story of this Black American
My History, I have learned to call me, Phenomenal
Immaculate I maybe, Gods child you see
But I am still a work in progress,
The sifting and combining, all is a process.
Growing to be a better me for the edification of His Kingdom
Come now see the many things that He has given.

Weeping may endure for a night but joy comes in the morning

I am not perfect… But saved with issues.

Lord thank you for delivering me from depression.

Lord thank you for delivering me from thoughts of suicide.

Lord thank you for delivering me from stupidity.

Lord thank you for delivering me from destruction.

Thank you for delivering me from me.

The worst enemy I ever had was myself, the worst enemy is me

I am not perfect… But saved with issues.

Angie Reames 2/21/2012

I won't be denied of what I deserve

Your ignorance your pettiness, your simplicity

Becomes my strength, my growth my expectancy

Motivated and encouraged because you're so simple minded

Thought I was dumb & you were catching me blind-sided.

Well think again, I know that it is all good when it's all God, I'm so hood

I know whose I am, where I stand and what I should… do

Not look at me and assume my kindness is weakness

Understand, I am saved with issues, my thug is just simply in remission

Grateful that He saved a wretch, Ha, Ecstatic that my name is Victory

The same things that make you laugh will make you cry, I can't continue to tell you that it's visible in Gods eyes

I refuse to let you interfere with what I already know I am expecting

I'm having contractions (the pain that I've bared), my water has broken (the tears that I've shed) I've dilated, (opened my heart and given it to God) ready for the birth of this blessing
So with my story and my struggles there are some things you should know
Let me remind you, I am focused, on a mission and determined to grow
I am screaming this to you it's not absurd, **I won't be denied of what I deserve**

Your ego and blatant lack of knowledge got you thinking you're in command
When the people have become stronger and prayed up to stand

Against all odds, no matter what you plan, without God you will plan to fail if you fail to plan,
I am here to tell you… there is no bigger God in you then it would be in the next man
Constantly degrading your fellow brothers because you aren't in command
When the people have been directed to give it to God and then stand
You are being used by the devil and don't even know it, your behavior is lame
You are merely a distraction, looking for someone else to blame
If only you weren't so caught up and you could see this transition

Perfect Imperfection   **Angie Taylor Reames**

Let me remind you, we are focused, determined to grow and on a mission

I am screaming this to you it's not absurd, **WE won't be denied of what we deserve**

Now here is how this reminder will end

You can forgive, stop trying to always reprimand

There is too much riding on our souls

No matter whose leader you choose to be, you have to learn to let go

Of the bitterness, the pettiness the anger and deceit

There is an issue that lies beneath all of our feet

But when we trust and believe that Gods Will shall be done

We won't hurt one another and our victory will be won

It's not that serious when the issue can be resolved

All because of a division everyone can't be on the same accord

But in case you can't feel this shift, just know that you're not the only one needing a lift

God is not pleased with the behavior of his people, so busy attacking one another that we forget about the issue

We are to remain focused, determined and ready for the mission

I am screaming this to you it's not absurd, **I won't be denied of what I deserve, You won't be denied of what you deserve, We won't be denied of what we deserve**

Angie Reames 4/24/2012 1/30/2013

Who Me? I'm different yeah I'm different

But you have been anointed by the Holy One and you all have knowledge (1 John 2:20) I am no better than the people out there in the world- I am just better off.... And if that thing that you see--- is the anointing on my life---Who me? I'm different yeah I'm different!

I wonder what Gods vision is of me? Naturally my perception attempts to the future I see- verses the God vision for me

Trying to find God in church politics and denominational differences- not knowing that that church purpose is to restore my identity and dignity

Haunted by my history that I keep carrying because somewhere I know that between these spots I am still haunted with past baggage

Yet to expose myself is the only way to trust- who I am because if we are to be anointed we must die like Jesus and that releases the God in us

I know that all this sifting and combining is a process so when I go through hell- it's just the anointing be combined and I grow- even I see the progress.

Yeah we are all God's children but we all look so different ya see- we have a different praise, assignment, gifts- In God I can't be you and you can't be me

Embracing who I am and who God designed me to be- You want to be holy? Become the best you that you can be.............. In Jesus Christ

The spirit of the Lord is upon me- He has sent me to proclaim liberty

Who me? I'm different yeah I'm different

Of all the misery that you have been through- Just know that the calling on your life is never over- God has a plan for you!

What is your conviction (passion)? How is it going to process you or me for the next step? I keep myself reminded that the ministry from your misery- is beneficial for the oppressed

And know that you or I should never be so spiritual that you forget your identity- so busy investing time into someone else and not enough time into me

When I'm failing and falling and trying to get to where I need to be- I crawl- I get up and get to that place meeting what God has for me

I cry out- Lord I'm sorry for allowing my flesh to take over my spiritual gain- because nothing in this world is comparable to a life without you- imagining chaos and pain

Salvation, deliverance, recovery, freedom, liberation - for all I will truly repent- & look at myself through the eyes of God- So God take me as I am

Because without God and this anointing over my life- I am no more than stuck and nothing is working because my plan is through flesh – just trite

I'm good- And we know that **all things work** together for **good** to them that love **God**, to them who are the called **according to** his **purpose**

Who me? I'm different yeah I'm different

Why is it so easy for us to give up on ourselves – we go through so much and blame the devil – When God is just strengthening us to be better through the hell

He never puts more on us than we can bear- yet we are so quick to fall instead of praise Him in the middle of it- and on Him- we can cast our care-

My greatest mercies are manifested from my worst miseries- This blessing wasn't easy- that's my story, learning to be the best me in He who strengthens me- being saved in reality

We give up on God – like He is man- when man will scandalize our very being but we have a God who forgives us and gives chance after chance- Does anyone agree in this?

Excuse me- I never said I was Holy but this chick right here will admit to being in Love with God- I am not perfect- But I am saved with issues… and for that I am proud- to serve HIM!

So when you see me smile- with my head held high- like there is no pain and no tears to cry- Just know that I am not conceited in this Christian Walk- but I know where I come from and where I could have been- But God

And all that He allows me to go through- I am thankful for the grace that has been given- and situations where I could have been dead- but grateful that even this wretch got saved instead because He never changed his mind about me-

So GOD I say thank you for ALL YOU'VE DONE FOR ME!!!

Who me? I'm different yeah I'm different--- Anointed-

Interior Circumstances also known as Inside Job

I declare and decree that your setbacks will be your comebacks
I declare and decree that your test will be your testimony
I declare and decree that your lost will be your found
I declare and decree that your crumble will be your crown

We have been so busy focusing on the imperfections that we don't see the great
Well, Greater is he that is in me than he that is in the world. So why are we in a broken state?
All because we trying to fix something that does not require our time,
So busy trying to fix yours and you fix mine, when you don't know my dull and you don't know my shine.

On me I have many bricks; on me I have many bruises. On me I have many titles, yet you continue to accuse me of being everything but a child of God… and because of it my pain become my handicap, holding myself hostage in this thing called life.

Perfect Imperfection   Angie Taylor Reames

Learn to hold it in and be someone else to make you smile, when my spirit is broken into pieces and my pride has become my style.
I am dealing with Interior Circumstances also known as Inside Job

Settling for the pickings, knowing that we aren't completely satisfied,
Because we so messed up from abuse, wickedness, church folk and lies.
Considering pleasing man, going through hell as a child of God, when we deserve more, but we too weary to reach,
 Pass the suffering from spiritual famish, listening to the pastor act and not preach, listening to the Reverend scream and not teach,

What God has positioned us to do in our life? We're focusing on our weakness and not our strength,
How strong are you? You know what you've been through and the distance in time and in length,
Scarred from neglect of things out of our control, we learn to adapt when we had a decision to just let them go
Now we trying to blame every one for the confusion that we have created, allowing our past to be present devastation

All this emotional destruction and leaders wanting to quit,
Came from within, that chaos we continue to battle with.
So instead of trying to fix you and you trying to fix me,

We got to work on the Inside Job… you got your issues and I got mine.

We are all created in the image of God,

Let's deal with the truth; let the facts stay facts,

I will deal with this…. You can deal with that

I won't be spiritually famished for things I can control

I am working on me, it's not that serious when I learn to let go

I may fall… but I will rise again

I declare and decree that the crumble will be my crown

I am dealing with Interior Circumstances also known as the Inside Job

4/18/2012 Angie Reames

Songwriter says **NO CHURCH IN THE WILD**- as the

wilderness.... In the Old Testament the people of Israel gathered in the wilderness. We the people are Gods church. Where we go... He will be there as well. He never leaves us. When our storms rage it helps us to appreciate the sunshine. So glad He doesn't give us what we say we want but He gives us exactly what we need. But even so... some lose focus and believe that they won't make it through the wilderness phase. Some lose focus and believe that they won't exist in the wild. Well God is everywhere... and if we are a church, we will be alive in the wild. We will make it... because God is omnipresent. No CHURCH in the WILD? I beg to differ...

Disempowered, helpless, things out of your control

Pride, Dignity, and self-respect- taking back everything that the devil stole

Dilemmas, darkness, heartache, neglect

Don't forget where you came from- grow as you reflect

Always weak and weary because of your position

Perfect Imperfection   **Angie Taylor Reames**

When you are faced with the same issues, causing chaos based on intuition

Settling and dumbing down because that is what the enemy expects

Personally I refuse to be spiritually ignorant and cling to my past regrets

Constantly making the minor things seem so major you see

Your situation isn't as major as you assume it to be

Worrying about the things that you have already prayed about

Then questioning God when your plans didn't pan out

Wondering where he is because you feeling so lost

He gave his only begotten son, Jesus died upon the cross

So that we could have life and we make excuses to live

Because we always manipulate want others to give, give, give

We cause so much pain on each other and then look for God to clean our mess

When the time we wasted on drama wasn't even worth our attention, just stress

Don't forget your purpose… Don't make chaos the ordinary descent

Perfect Imperfection   **Angie Taylor Reames**

Know that you are never alone in life, God is omnipresent

He is always there… through your storm, your struggle, your weariness, your life

He is everywhere; you'd be a fool to believe that there ain't no church in the wild.

Believe in yourself… God does. He didn't create no mess.

I am my sisters keeper... and I pray that she is

mine... so many times we pour into our sisters expecting them to have the same love or respect for us and they have a different motive then what we have and vice versa... we miss out on what God is telling us to do stressing the approval from our sisters- and our sister end up being our haters- yet our haters become our biggest motivators--- but how many of you know that we are to love one another... we are to pray for one another ... If we prayed for one another more and stop finding minor things to make major then we won't feel like we need to prey on one another... this is for my sisters... and this is for your sisters... ladies repeat... **I am my sisters keeper... we need God.**

She said that we were sisters and I trusted her so I believed when she called me her sibling and we laughed like it was our **last** but now this chick is **mad** because I'm growing in God and she **stabs** me in my **back**, only for me to realize that genuine sisters shouldn't act like **that**.

We could talk about everything and I never felt **alone**, I could cry about anything and her shoulders I was **on**, I never went **without** but now my name from her **mouth** screams lies heartaches and all the secrets I shared are starting to come **out**.

My sister has turned into my number one hater, not **right**. All because I am growing in **Christ** and you would think she would be happy but I think her **shout** was a **pout** to get attention, I've learned this chick and I'm all 'sistered' **out**.

See it shouldn't take war to bring an end to the **pain**, because by shunning my sister what will I **gain**?

So many women have gotten so caught up in church folk **mentality** that we look for daddy in man's approval and that is just small minded church **technicality**.

What makes you think that someone else doesn't deserve the right to be **saved**? God accepted you, forgave you and your still digging your own **grave**?

Don't be a sister, covered in hater's wool, pretending for selfish **reasons**... Because there is a shift in the atmosphere, it's a new time and a different **season**.

I dare you pretend to be grace when someone needs to be spiritually **fed**, because you so busy wanting to feel like the only child of God, and end up catching hell **instead**.

Knocking one another down because you think you're whispering is a spiritual **gift**, there ain't nothing holy about gossip, just lies and secret that you still battle **with**.

Struggling to cover up your nonsense and become a thorn in someone else's **side**, Filled with heartache, neglect, and your heart too cold to love, yet you hide behind that little **pride**.

Attempting to love when all that you display is **fake**... well here let me tell you ... IT AINT about you... I'm doing what I do for Him... your shenanigans I can no longer **take**.

I love you because you were also created by **Him**, but if you want to put me down in Jesus name... then you hang with the church folk, I can't get deal with **them**.

My heart will always love you and my spirit will always be my sister's **keeper**, but I pray that you find God and stop investing in approval from the **people**.

And God- I'm not saying that I am better then the next sister in the **pew**, but my works is not done for man, I just want to be closer to **you**

See we all have our past, our background that's our **history**, that place where we get our ministry strengthened from our **misery**…

I am not perfect, saved with issues, I am learning as I grow in God's **grace**, with endurance I must remain faithful and focused to run this **race**

Yet- I battle the flesh when the spirit is the **truth**, becoming stressed through test and demeanor is calm to uncouth – I just want to be closer to **you**

Torn between where I should be and where I need to **go** because I seem so unworthy compared to others that I **know**

But God said you are my child and Pastor Barnes said your misery will be your **ministry**, so when you are broken just trust God to bring you through **this**.

God love me- NO matter the storm that rage in my **life, I** must be strong enough to have faith in Him and everything will be **alright**.

So even in my broken state, I will try to **maintain**, I have nothing else to lose but I know there is so much more to **gain**…. Some days I wish my sister wasn't so judgmental and understood my **pain**.

So to her I say I am sorry for anything I **did**, an apology is one thing but we all need to learn to **forgive**

Please accept this for anything I may have **done**… let's not be a hindrance to one another trying to get to know the **son**.

So I will end by saying: When I am down to my last and on my knees I will **fall**… even my sister who has left me… strengthens me and my wretchedness confirms that I am Equipped for the **Call**… I am my Sisters Keeper… We need God!

9/20/2012

SOMEWHERE THERE IS A LEADER IN YOU

Somewhere there is a father and a son.

Somewhere there is a dad with a bottle and a son with a gun

Somewhere there is gang violence on the street corner

Somewhere there is a dad trying to be a mother to a daughter,

Somewhere there is a mother looking for a mate to help raise that boy

Somewhere there is a father wanting to be home and not deployed

Somewhere there is a child being neglected by a dad

All because he can't be a man, so he abuses the child when he gets mad.

Somewhere there is a kid on drugs

Because mama angry that daddy left and no one never gave that child a hug, Somewhere there a child just wanting to be loved

Somewhere there is a child with nowhere to live

Perfect Imperfection   **Angie Taylor Reames**

Because daddy said get out because he has no more to give

Somewhere there is a kid needing a church home

But the local drug dealers took em' in first by providing a cell phone

Somewhere there is a community of babies needing someone to care

But the church folk so busy judging that they aren't even there

Somewhere just somewhere there is a boy needing a guide, because he is trying to be a man, his dad died.

And we have men who have experienced the same things, but afraid of the truth, so they hide behind their pride

Just somewhere, somewhere there is work that has to be done

Because there is a man who has to help these boys get to know the Son

And here we have guys who claim to be men, who know what is needed because they're leaders within

Men who would rather set back instead of step up

To help the boy become a man before he screws his life up

Men who can use what they have been through to help heal the pain of another

But remain in bondage, afraid to share their story, looking crazy because now their son is another man's lover.

Men… there is a leader in you. Don't let anyone tell you any different.

7/7/2012

What type of seed are you?

Spiritual Tubal Ligation got you devastated underestimating yourself thinking you can't bring life into your situation… What type of seed are you nurturing and questioning yourself when even a tubal in flesh is reversible.

Listen closely… Your greatest fear is not that you will fail because you have done that time after time, got up tried again and still prevailed.

Your supreme fear is the scheme of your mind trying to conquer your dream when through your faith you are capable of anything yet you are afraid to succeed.

SO you allow yourself to plant the bad seeds and blame everyone else when you have spiritually blasphemed where you need to be

Simple. You have the ability to speak life over your situation. You are capable of planting that seed and watching its manifestation on your life.

What is the purpose of planting in dead ground looking for a birthing of something that isn't worth it… speaking life over dead areas that aren't working to grow you into who you need to be

Fertilizing the present with spiritual gifts and no life in it, change your surroundings your history is just stiff just like the dead things in it, you're nurturing misery

Learn to let go of the things that hold you hostage bounded by oppression from the very ones who seed into you for their growth the most only for you to realize you shouting over them in idolatry, it ain't even the Holy Ghost.

Whipped with words so that you can be viewed as ignorant to folk, well they ignorant too. Because it's not for everyone to know the same things that everyone else knows.

You aren't dumb so don't dumb yourself down just to lift up others so they can shine… it's really about God and a good leader is produced after its own kind.

We tend to miss out on what God is actually blessing us with because we let flesh do the inspecting, well we aren't to be so judgmental, what if God saw our mess and each time did inspecting just so he could do rejecting and we can't sacrifice instead we neglecting.

We so busy pointing fingers like our growth was done overnight and neither were you born saved; you just religiously constipated looking up tight.

SO I need you to hear this and hear this loud and clear… Don't hold onto producing your seeds, there are people that are spiritually hungry waiting on people like us to go feed.

Don't worry yourself if you find yourself surrounded by negativity, because God has a purpose for you and your seed will grow regardless of what season you are in

God has a purpose for you and your seed, your gift, your talent he will make room for, don't think it's over for you just because you're stuck between two closed doors. Stay in the word and give nourishment to what you have in your heart… even God puts back the broken when we have been torn apart… SO I ask you what type of seed are you?

10/5/12

THEY SAY, YOU SAY, I SAY!

They say giving your life to Jesus is the epitome of all things that are worth living

For and in me he will create a new creature but they didn't tell me about that bridge called hell season that I had to cross to get where I need to be;

So even in my off season I question this personification of what man makes perfect and I question if I am worth it

Because even my soul needs a rebirthing

And my spirit has been drained because **they say** that all the tears I cried would be washed away

And all the pain that I endure would come to an end... I keep allowing myself to focus on the positive things - **they say**

this walk gets hard & I'll need somebody to answer my questions and I'll need somebody to believe in me **& they say** just talk to YOU and everything would be ok... but now I'm at point A and clueless of how to get to point B

In you I find myself being whipped with scripture no explanation by they who claim to know You GOD, and lead by the people with the finger in the air, no smile and a cold heart, attempting to usher

Their way into my spirit and I still stumble over the pew next to the sister who wants me to dress a certain way before I can be accepted by you

My soul has been murdered and assaulted by church folk because they wear Sunday attire and attack new babes in you because they have been warming pews since the very beginning and claim to know God more than me this can't be truth

They say I am a nobody because they judge me and my sins are more critical because they were forgiven by God centuries ago, and refuse to teach me what way to go, stuck in church politics and worship ain't even in it, and through it all my soul continues to die and O YEAH they ain't never told no lie they ain't never told no lie

My heart aches after the attack of the enemy because I know better but don't do better because the church folk have taught me to sit back and shut up; and just wing with sister so and so… what they call just agree and go with the flow

Generation after generation abiding by these same rules and following these same guidelines when they have nothing to do with being saved, just based on what **they say**

Well God I confess with my heart, that I want to be CLOSER to you and I don't want to be manipulated by church folk who rape my spirit with belligerence and hold me hostage, in slave spirituality, because **they say**

I ain't perfect, but you say I am worth it and you say I deserve it, and I know that you love me in spite of me and **you say**!

God **You say** that you will supply every one of my needs according to your riches in glory by Christ Jesus, and I believe in this promise & I keep myself reminded of you- reminded

You are an omnipresent God, there with me when they say I wasn't nothing, No one can take your place, You have made provision for our salvation by His grace through faith, your grace is sufficient... **YOU SAY**

That your children will not be overtaken with temptation and assure that a way will be provided, I may have fallen short but I have a GOD of an-other chance, in HIM I will confide in... and **YOU SAY**

That all things work together for the good to those that Love and serve you... even in my HELL SEASON when I was trying to cross

the bridges, you still remained TRUE, turned my PAIN into
PRAISE, **YOU SAY**

That those who believe in Jesus and are baptized for the forgiveness-
of sins will be saved and God **you say** we shall have eternal life.

Forget what THEY SAY- I want the truth, the truth in what YOU
SAY GOD!

I say- I won't be a hostage by generational curses, with negative
spirits larking ready to rape me of my love and knowledge of my
FATHER, spiritual molestation will no longer appear in my life and
I am no longer a puppeteer of fear... I won't be destroyed in Jesus
name... (TAKE ME TO THE KING) because God **I say** "I GIVE
MYSELF AWAY"

8/30/2012

What if you really knew the truth about me... would you judge me?

Often times we forget who we really are because we get mentally handicapped by society…. Trying to do things to please other people and we end up hiding things are doing things that are not pleasing … then struggle to embrace our sanity… trying to find who we really are… or should I say who God has designed us to be. May this bless you and may you know that regardless of who you think you are in flesh… that God has so much more for you--- you are a child of God and that is no doubt regardless of who choose to judge you.

What if I said I was in love with the extra stride in my step and the way my feet hit the floor and the way my lip gloss popped and the way I held my spot in the arch of my back and the brightness of my eyes especially when I smiled…all a lie- what If I told you I was in love but heartbroken with insecurity of what others really thought of me…

What if I said I walked with my head held high because I was confident enough not to look down and I am proud of my accomplishments and I know that the room gets quiet when I enter because the walls just have to whisper of my beauty… what If I told you I was afraid so I pretended to be strong because I felt weak compared to others…

What if you really knew the truth about me…would you judge me?

What if I make you laugh because deep down I'm sad and I cover up all my past mistakes with today's fad and I make everything look easy because mentally I was pressing on when things got bad and instead of solving my issues – I just ignored them and ran and got out of the way when they came full speed slapping me in my face

What If I told you I was in a bad relationship but chose to stay because I was thinking about how others felt and not taking into consideration what was happening to me because I just wanted to look pretty but the internal bruising was worse than any that the flesh could get. Inflicting myself with hatred, anger and bitterness.

What if you really knew the truth about me… would you judge me?

What if I told you I drank liquor and smoked cigarettes daily to get the pain out of the way and when all the laughter ceased and the good times ended the pain was back because it never left. The drunken laughter was there to suppress the bitter pain that I keep allowing myself to experience in the situation that chose to stay in

What if I told you I was turned on by small compliments because I didn't see my own beauty not even skin deep? What if I told you I was raised in a single parent home with a mother who made sure we were never without but all my friends thought I was a military brat because I lived near a base but it was always in a trailer park would you think I'm trash?

What if you really knew the truth about me... would you judge me?

What if I told you I battled with insecurity and some days I don't even trust me. What if I told you I had to get on medication because life got so stressful that I wanted to take it away... end all the pain and all the things that were pressuring me to be the best me that I can be and I almost failed the test because I just didn't want to be?

What if I told you that I attempted to be perfect because I was ignorant to what I was really worth- but the perfection was to be accepted by others because they looked so happy and I was unaware that they had a story because I really thought that ALL bad things were only happening to me- blind to the truth- saw what I wanted to see

What if you really knew the truth about me... would you judge me?

See I know that what is coming is better than what has been. I know that all the things that I have been through have only strengthened me into who I am- and all the present chaotic situations are preparing me for what is to be. I know that now,

I know that I am beautiful- I was created by GOD… I am fearfully and wonderfully made by a creator who makes no mistakes… I am secure with who I am and where He needs me to be. I am not perfect but being saved in who He designed me to be… I know that now,

See I know that when everything starts falling apart and it seems like the devil has everything that concerns me on his to do list that God will turn it around for my good. And I shall, will and am going to minister through my misery… I know that now

I know that I am royalty and God gets all the glory. I am ok if you choose to judge me--- because you will have to answer to HIM for that… I am a child of a king… know that now!

Of all the things that I have done… the lies that I have told… the things that I have stolen… be it loyalty or trust. HE forgave me… He still forgives… I have changed… into what God is sculpting me to be…

He has and is blessing me with more than I could ever imagine--- I thank God for my husband, my children, my family, my friends, my inspirational motivators and grace, I thank God for mercy… I thank

God for you… if you knew me then--- would you thank Him for me now?

I am a woman of God – fearfully and wonderfully made- reporting for duty as I present what I represent! The God in me- gracefully ministering through my misery- exposing my story and giving God the glory as I Present what I Represent! A CHILD OF A KING!

SO what if you really knew the truth about me… would you judge me?

2/11/13 Angie Reames

Beautiful Women Who Do Beautiful Things!

Whether it's a trophy we have received for doing something great!

Or maybe a certificate of recognition for stepping out on faith.

It could be a hug that we gave to someone who was going through hurt and pain!

Or maybe the time when we guided someone to Jesus so they could have a chance to stand.

We are beautiful women who do beautiful things!

Whether it's the time we rubbed and kissed the bruise on our baby's knee,

Or maybe when we prayed for our troops who were being all that they could be.

It 62 be the flowers that we sent a friend, who was having a rough day,

Or maybe the time when we faced hard times & on our knees we went to pray.

We are beautiful women who do beautiful things!

Perfect Imperfection   **Angie Taylor Reames**

How about the time when we made dinner for someone who needed to be fed,

Or prayed for someone who had been confined to a bed?

It could be the smile from our lips that makes a person feel better,

Sometimes it's the words that we may put in a card or the love we place in a letter!

We are beautiful women who do beautiful things!

Whether it's the time when God blessed us to give birth,

Or the time we ministered to someone who didn't know their worth!

It's the times when we stand firm and give God all the praise!

When we can understand the difference between good & evil ways!

Making it look easy to be strong when inside we are feeling so feeble

Trusting a God we have never seen but with faith we continue to believe

Grateful for mercy and Thankful for grace

Enduring each passing day-pressing on in this race

We are beautiful women who do beautiful things!!

Today we honor women! We recognize females! We celebrate beauty!

Whether it's the smile on our face or the warmth in our heart! We are beautiful Women who do Beautiful Things!

It could be the song sang from our lips or the story that tells our struggles! We are beautiful Women who do Beautiful Things!

It could be the sassiness when we point a finger or the humbleness in the tone of our voice! We are beautiful women who do beautiful things!!

Whether it's the lip gloss on our lips and shadow on our eyes or the virtue around our neck and the confidence in our stride! We are beautiful Women who do beautiful things!!

Today we celebrate beautiful women in faith! We celebrate beautiful women who know that without God we are lost and with him we have direction. Today we celebrate life, we celebrate love, we celebrate beauty, we celebrate women and the beautiful things that we do to keep our house in order- today we celebrate mothers!

The March at the Mount

We could sit here and mumble and hum old negro spirituals

And reminisce on the tv box when it was black and white and be intimidated by the colors that we are dark

We could stop in our tracks and never press on to the journey

And take every thing into consideration that our ancestors have done but never take the history made and learn from it

We could wear the scars that our ancestors wore like scarves around our neck noose in the spirit and broken before the poor

And be rich in intelligence but choose not to deliver it dumbing ourselves down for imperfect people also known as hypocrites

We could stand in a field and not have a career based on a percentage rate given by politics in a race

And look at the world with blurred vision because we don't want to believe in Gods amazing grace

We could pretend to be ignorant to the freedom that God has given us

And be held hostage with our slave mentality until ashes are ashes and dust to dust

We could be so small in stature and reveal only our passions through evident of disaster

And be a victim in life to everything we're trying to rid, while we're afraid to be caught in the rapture

Well we could be so many things but I'd rather be free... from every

Negative thing that imperfectionist may say about me and I'd rather write my vision and make it plain like the bible says and declare that I have dream like MLK and be freed from chains that attempt to keep me bounded in oppression

I'd rather be free from depression. And smiling from the victories won from the fights that my forefathers won and praising the Lord, from the rising of the sun for ALL that He has done for me.

So yeah ...

We could sit here and mumble and hum old negro spirituals- but be thankful of the blessings God has given us

We could stop in our tracks and never press on to the journey – but only if God says the process is to sit still for the race ahead and its endurance

We could wear the scars that our ancestors wore like scarves around our neck noose in the spirit and broken before the poor – but even if we fall down, we must be encouraged to get back up and be stronger than before

We could stand in a field and not have a career based on a percentage rate given by politics in a race- or be the percentage rate that proves to be great- we're blessed in the city, on the hill, comin out and going in

We could pretend to be ignorant to the freedom that God has given us or live gracefully and believe that Jesus was born,lived, died and rose again that we may have life more abundantly

We could be so small in stature and reveal only our passions through evident of disaster or be passionate about the gifts that God has given us and reveal our greatest through the actions of our rapture

Well we could be so many things but I'd rather be free... Grateful that He did it just for me... and proud to celebrate the birth of a man who fought for equality. Martin Luther King Jr spoke out for justice for African Americans, for an end to racial discrimination, to the laws that embodied it and the many subtle, unconscious behaviors

Martin Luther King, Jr. did many things to bring greater equality to America and to ensure civil rights for all people regardless of race. The major things that Martin Luther King did were to:

Bring publicity to major civil rights activities and efforts

Emphasize and encourage the importance of non-violent protest and resistance.

Provide leadership to the African-American civil rights movement

Just a little done by Martin Luther King, Jr- I'd rather be free and celebrate his birth this day while I proclaim I have a dream and I'll let my freedom ring.

This may not be the March on Washington, but I dare you to proclaim your freedom and be your best self and March at the Mount… Free at Last, Free at Last.. thank God almighty we are Free at Last.

1/14/2014 Angie Taylor Reames

The Silence of Pain is Deadly

What if it was inclusive that the pain is perpetual and extremely threatening?

Trying to dismiss the thought of what has happened- the past

The neglect that stalked reality or insanity in its mere presence

Because honestly the silence of pain is deadly! I'll say it again

What if it was inclusive that the pain is perpetual and extremely threatening?

Trying to dismiss the thought of what has happened- the past

The neglect that stalked reality or insanity in its mere presence

Because honestly the silence of pain is deadly!

Why do we hurt and attempt to cover it up

Becoming unaware of who we are to our self because our flesh is all screwed up

Why do we allow others to see our bright side when darkness never went away?

Attempting to be coy and let our dark hide- think it will just stray

Because honestly the silence of pain is deadly!

Argumentative with our spiritual self because we got caught up in the wrong confusion

Failing to treat life as a gift- we just living on hope and getting twisted in illusion- nothing but delusion

All have sin and fallen short- but we treat life like we don't have a chance to be Consecrated- set apart

Why do we feel that hoarded pain will birth anything except things to be torn apart?

Because honestly the silence of pain is deadly!

Distorted criticism from every mechanism because others tend to look down on the weak

But others hurt too – we all tend to bruise- viral melancholy because the atmosphere was always bleak

The pointing of fingers compared to patrolmen trying to point me in the right direction

But why must one endure so much pain- when others seem to get an eternity of affection

Because honestly the silence of pain is deadly!

What must I do to be considered ... into the kingdom? TRUST GOD AND HIS PLAN FOR ME>>> Believe in He who strengthens me when all others think I am too weak... cry out and make known who it is that I am... because the silence of pain is deadly. 2/23/13

I could cry a river for the pain that I have endured but the loudest cry is the scream that I have held in feeling broken and this pain I can't take no more

Carrying these bricks each with their own special name- stress, depression, suicidal thoughts, overwhelmed, worn and more

And every attempt to throw them down only results in another being thrown in my direction and to dodge it is impossible but I find myself in fetal position- stretch to the floor.

Father I stretch my hands to thee you're the only help I know. I have given it to you all the worrying and pressure that days beginning brings must cease

I am looking for my morning because I have been told that it'll all be over in the morning and yet I'm here living my life in the state of mourning

Crying because I have yet to assume the position of smiling and life seems like death hanging in the darkness of each time I close my eyelids

And I am wondering can these bones live? Can the bones that my flesh covers be covered in spirit and the truth in knowing that Jesus Lives?

Lives in me and my anointing cries for more of YOU! Afraid to express my inner misery because I don't want to seem weak when others depend on my for strength

I need it too but I am so sure that they can't see pass the imaginary S on my chest- it's not super powers- My S is for Savior because I need you just as them

Life has me in a seasonal state of being led blind through hell fast and furious rest in peace Paul Walker afraid to close my eyes because the death angel is working overtime

I will be freed from all this negative energy that is trying to capture me in its spiritual blasphemy and the enemy tries to get credit for where God is taking me

In the end I just want to be freed more of you and less of me.

My body suffering from the aftermath of procedural side effects and my temple is to be used for you so I am trying to be mindful and not neglect

The fact is I'm suffering from capacity overload, being torn and pulled in every direction, mentality on spiritual warfare and mind ready to explode

Into a thousand pieces because what good am I for my family if I am not capable of being me for me and what if my friends don't understand my scream

Because they assume that my smile is an invite for their pain when in actuality I'm covering up the emotions that bring me down from the time that I've used my misery as ministry to help them climb

Get up I have to tell myself. TRY again you're just a step away from your spiritual upgrade because everything that you're going through is only preparing you to endure the process

And God I know you got me even when I want to stay down and hide from everyone including myself. Not everyone can understand my pain because instead of listening some just want to start a plan

To fix what I have has to start with me… but that same hug I give sometimes I just need to receive. But I am aware that I shall be stronger,

Stronger with each tear, more faithful with each fear and a better me than what I was yesterday. IF YOU ONLY KNEW

Lord I just need you to make me over- I have found myself screaming internally and smiling externally but Lord I don't want to be a victim of screaming faith from a safe place because the truth is I don't feel safe in this place unless I have you.

There are indeed levels to this game called life and I am stuck between waiting on my next re-up because it's not over for me

As many times I wanted to assume the position and quit- be gone and get it over with. My cries- my scream- these suicidal thoughts- God keeps waking me up and I ain't got time for that.

God I need thee! Every hour I need thee, my screams are bottled in waiting for that escape but they are so powerful I need them out in a safe place

Even the people who say they love me I'm afraid they won't understand my cry. Because what I have to express continues to eat me alive- who wants to give the committal

I was told that I am to live full and die empty. Well I am full. Full of the pain and empty of not being consoled or understood. So I poetically express my pain through the ministry that GOD has given me

Others tell me that they are dealing with life like I don't have to live. Trying to remember everything for everyone else and not able to stop and understand even how I feel

I want to start over fresh. Give in to all the pressure and save any sanity that I have left.

But where am I to begin when all I have in me is a scream- the silence of pain is deadly- Is it possible to rest in peace and still live.

12/05/2013 Angie Reames

Hello Pain

Hello pain. Here it is I come to you again. I am confronting you for attempting to steal my joy. I will not complain because my flesh has allowed me to do that occasionally until I snapped back into reality… realizing that my father is greater than that and worrying should not be second nature but hey I am human. Hey pain I refuse to allow you to have my life. Today I will take it back just like I took it back from depression when I was fighting tears, in a fetal position crying to my nightmares as if they cared and literally pulling my hair strand by strand because the sadness that I displayed on my face couldn't be erased because I was unaware of disgrace that the enemies tried to throw in my space. The constant preying that they attempted to construct against my life only failed because the anointed on my life is not to be toiled with. Hey enemy you can't play two roles… either you're a child of a King or you're choosing to be hells servant. I shall not be moved. I will stand and see that's where I am. Hello pain

Here it is I come to you again-I see you for who you are- I refuse to claim what the enemy is attempting to wave in my face as a noose.

God wants me to be victorious the enemy wants me to be a fool but before I allow anyone to hurt my heart or batter my spirit. You best believe I won't make any decisions without God in it. So if you see me bending you won't see me break- I may fall because every comforter will have scars. I was wounded and may still have a little damage but hello pain- I'm a soldier and my God won't give me anything I couldn't handle.

Hello pain- the attempt to make me feel like my shivers were permanent and this spiritual warfare was torment is only God preparing me for what's to come and I will be prepared for what He has for me ahead of this journey- I have been talked about, looked down on, mistreated, told the truth on, judged and here I am- the pain of life's daily hell tried to remove me- preying on my gifts and trying to break my family. Using coins to rob me with its spiritual blasphemy- staring and whispering-but the devil can't move me. My God is bigger but what keeps you here?

Even the face that you attempt to be an attraction- is negative but you are not a distraction to me- because hell has no fury to a woman that has already won.

Hello pain- even this damage is beginning to heal and I will shout to the hills from where all of my help comes. Because that thumbprint that He has placed on my life represents a calling- I don't have to explain it to you- but the more battles that I win the more victories I proclaim and the lower my valley experience the higher I rise in Jesus name. I won't be denied of what I deserve. Your weakness has been revealed and you shall reap what you have sown. Hello Pain. Hello Pain. I am not afraid, I am not defeated, and I am not tired. I am stronger- although you attempted to mistreat me. I am a child of King. Hello Pain, you've been defeated- game over!

5/20/2014

Scars

My silent cries are rarely seen because I am so adept at adapting to my surroundings and looking like I should be brilliant and perfect in front of you people who love God and sin as me. Unaware of my cries and I smile because it's beautiful while my pain resides behind the silence of the lies that are hard to be left unspoken and yet on a good day I strive to be perfected by the scriptures and strengthened by what is fed to me because even I know that the silence of pain is deadly but I fight to have faith in a God I have never seen but aware that He has never failed me and He believes in me. So when I cried silently it's because the Father can hear me and I cast my worries on Him because He cares for me- even when man tend to lie on me, mistreat me and emotionally batter me- I may seem frail but He still believes in me- and while you can't see my scars they are proof that I went to war with the enemy but I won because God fights with me and I declare it victoriously.

My silent cries are rarely seen because honestly I am embarrassed of what you may think. We all have a past and through this poetic ministry I am to share my history to help someone else from my experienced pain and my hell and misery. Hypocritically I don't seem addicted to a lot of things but I cuss like a sailor just to get my emotions freed but because some tend to judge- they don't see the

God in me… or maybe it's because my history is being used against me as spiritual blaspheme- I never claimed to be perfect but in a world of church folk and folk playing church I don't know any other way to be freed other than being me and yet I am worried about what you may think ya see---

My scars are silent cries rarely seen because I battle with insecurities- I am not the size of a super model and I no longer fit the size three.. My hair is being invaded by hints of grey and I maybe young but I am mature beyond my age so I don't know what pretty is because compliments are no longer given or perhaps I don't receive them. Illness makes me feel senile and the feature that I once adored is now the hole to my soul because my eyes speak loud when I can't take no more. Temporary insanity when my mind was being attacked by the enemy rescued by prayer ya see and the image in the mirror made me scream at reality and cried silently because no one understood my cries of secrecy. The secret is I don't want to live in this capsule that holds reality- yet reality produces the past and in my future I will minister to someone who deals with the same things as me and at that point my misery will be my history but until then my scars are silent cries rarely seen…

This pain- heartbreak and heartache and things that I can't handle but I can't run from either. Responsibilities that I have been blessed with but trying to be freed from because I just want to be freed from stress and yet alone can't understand why I feel like I am less then what I am because no one understands the depths of the pain and the desires of my soul to be freed. Rest stop doing so much you're only one person you can't keep going but who is there to help me. Who can I run to when I need it… everyone want me to sit and rest but no one wants to relieve me so I can be freed from the hell that I feel keeps pressing itself in my spirit-my mind my mind in my mind. Pretending to listen to the pain and then add onto your bricks with their insanity and killing me mentally silently with the weight off of their issues and I am TIRED and I have SCARS. It's hard to take time for yourself -when I'm the wall that holds up everyone who is depending on me and it's hard to hold in the tears when I'm stressed so I laugh really hard to release all the stress. I've been told that laughter is good for the soul… but it doesn't cover up the scars. SCARS…. Everyone has battles fights with pain and reality, neglect, stress, frustration, confusion, relationships, loneliness, heartbreak, heartache, pornography, adultery, alcoholism, mental abuse, physical abuse, gambling, racism, depression, fornication, drug abuse, capacity overload, religion-we all battle with something. Perhaps your Silent Cries are Rarely Seen! Cry.

Perfect Imperfection   **Angie Taylor Reames**

My silent cries are rarely seen because I am so adept at adapting to my surroundings and looking like I should be brilliant and perfect in front of you people who love God and sin as me. Unaware of my cries and I smile because it's beautiful while my pain resides behind the silence of the lies that are hard to be left unspoken and yet on a good day I strive to be perfected by the scriptures and strengthened by what is fed to me because even I know that the silence of pain is deadly but I fight to have faith in a God I have never seen but aware that He has never failed me and He believes in me. So when I cried silently it's because the Father can hear me and I cast my worries on Him because He cares for me- even when man tend to lie on me, mistreat me and emotionally batter me- I may seem frail but He still believes in me- and while you can't see my scars they are proof that I went to war with the enemy but I won because God fights with me and I declare it victoriously.

Silent Cries Rarely Seen- my SCARS and I shall cry aloud because I know God still walks with me.

6/25/2014

Closing

I would first like to thank God for the gift that He has blessed and trusted me with. All the praises and Honor belong to him.

I thank the Pastor of our house, Mr. Antowine Reames for loving me the best way he knows how and respecting the calling on my life. I am thankful to him for his words of encouragement and his prayers. I am thankful to him for understanding when I needed a quiet space to meditate and get in the word. Thank you for inviting me to church, thank you for helping me to understand that I didn't have to be perfect to be saved. I am thankful to him for not running when I am on my God assignment and going through the pressing-for loving me the best way he knows how and respecting the calling on my life-for being strong enough to stay when my emotions ran free. I am thankful that he never judged me, he respects me and he loves me unconditionally.

I thank God for my children, who are so patient even when they have no idea what mood I am in on certain days. For believing in me when I don't believe in myself. But I am more thankful to God for keeping me. My children are the ones who keep me lifted, motivated, rounded and I just want to say thank you- I don't know where I would be without them- Shakaila, Kalen and Hannah are my everything and they continue to inspire me.. Thank you to Keiara, Keenen and Antowine Xavier for allowing me to be a part of their life and motivating me to be better. To my mama, Maggie Pearson and my dad, James Taylor Jr. … you all are the best and I am extremely grateful to have you all as my parents. I have never been without and that is because you always made sure I had what I needed.

Thank you to my brother, Richard Kulade Washington for writing his raps and letting me get in on the chorus with a poem, after a beat was thrown behind it. I looked up to you then, thank you, my first male best friends. You have made such an impact on my life and I am not sure you are aware of it but I appreciate you.

I would like to thank my "Thing 2", Cedric Dion McDuffie for always knowing exactly what to say when I felt like quitting and loving me when he didn't have to and for making sure our friendship and his support is always "SOLID".

Thank you to Pastor Andre C Barnes for being the Godfather of my poetry ministry. If it wasn't for him giving me an opportunity to minister through poetry when I didn't see it for myself, I wouldn't be in this season of my life.

Thank you to Pastor Travis Laws for being that praying brother and pushing me when I feel like pausing by encouraging me to keep going.

I am thankful to Jennifer Johnson Cook for being my "SOUL" sister, My Jenny Lynn and my spiritual sister- always praying and encouraging me. She inspires me to be great!

I am thankful to Cherie Buckman, my sister for our life changing trip to Galax, VA and for loving me all these years.

I am thankful to Shirley Reames McDonald for being my Ride or Die, my sister from another mother, my sister in law and ready to roll with a sister.

Thank you Michelle Fedd for blessing me with idea for my title, my beautiful sister you rock and I love you!

Thank you to Elizabeth Gary for seeing something in me and being obedient to God. I thank her for believing in me and seeding into my life and my ministry. I appreciate her for letting me know that "It's OK".

There are so many people that I appreciate. I love each of you and I thank you for supporting my ministry. God bless you and continue to smile… You can't run from that thumbprint.

About the Author

Angie Taylor Reames has been writing poetry since she was fourteen years old. She believes that the best way to find healing is to be transparent and minister from her misery. Angie is from South Carolina and grew up thinking that she had to be perfect (for imperfect people). With time, lessons, experience and maturity later in life Angie realized that she is perfectly imperfect and she is exactly who God created her to be. Angie wrote this book as it was a valuable necessity in inspiring others in Christ. She enjoys ministering through poetry as it is a way of motivating others and uplifting the Word of God and encouraging others to be their best self. She loves to share her smile with others because you never know when others are having a bad day.

1 Corinthians 15:10

"I am what I am by God's grace, and God's grace hasn't been for nothing. In fact, I have worked harder than all the others—that is, it wasn't me but the grace of God that is with me."

Pure Thoughts Publishing, LLC

www.PureThoughtsPublishingllc.com

www.ingramcontent.com/pod-product-compliance
Lightning Source LLC
LaVergne TN
LVHW011335080426
835513LV00006B/367